Rocky and Roxanne
Roadrunner

by Pamela Robbins
Illustrated by Eduardo Paj

Copyright © 2022 by Family Tree Publishing

All rights reserved. No part of this book may be reproduced or used in any manner without written permission of the copyright owner except for the use of quotations in a book review. For more information contact: info@familytree.pub

Author Pamela Robbins

Book design by Eduardo Paj

ISBN: 978-1-957308-03-6

Library of Congress Control Number: 2021925242

https://familytree.pub

This book is dedicated to my children and grandchildren.
May the love of learning and nature be ever present and preserved.

Rocky and Roxanne Roadrunner are at home in the Southwestern desert.

Here they run and play, flit, flitter, hop…and sway.

All day they eat bugs, lizards, snakes and spiders
as they wander the grasses in the warm breeze.

When they run and play,
flit, flitter, hop...and sway,
they find a beautiful
Palo Verde tree along their way.

Together they start to build.
Rocky brings sticks and small twigs

one by one

**BACK AND FORTH
BACK AND FORTH,**

He runs, flits and flitters, hops and sways,
taking them to the bottom of that tree.

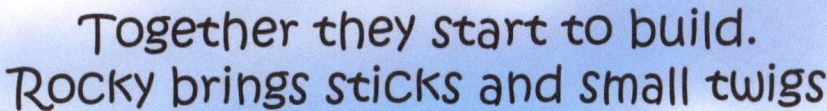

Roxanne takes the sticks and twigs

one by one
BACK AND FORTH
BACK AND FORTH

She carefully, flits and flitters, hops
and sways up and down the tree trunk.

UP AND DOWN

UP AND DOWN

layering them on a branch
of that Palo Verde tree.

Rocky runs as fast as he can
as he flits, flitters, hops and sways
bringing more grasses and leaves,
feathers and weeds to make their nest soft.

"What is this?
A snakeskin left behind.
It is perfect for our nest.
We'll use this."

Little by little
day by day

Rocky and Roxanne build their nest together,
they are doing their best, with no time to rest,
as they flit, flitter, hop and sway along the way.

When it was done,
Roxanne nestled in and laid five eggs!

She stays on her nest
and keeps the eggs warm all day.

Rocky trades places with her
and keeps the eggs warm all night.

For three long weeks, day and night,
they sit and dream, as they work as a team,
all nestled safely in the Palo Verde tree.

Suddenly,
the eggs begin to crack and just like that...

Rocky and Roxanne have five baby chicks,
all peeping and cheeping, calling for food.

All day, Rocky brings food to his hungry baby chicks while Roxanne stays close.

Rocky runs as fast as he can to find lizards and snakes, insects and spiders for his chicks to eat.

They grow and grow,
and soon the chicks leave the nest.
They flit, flitter, hop... and sway,
looking for food along the way.

They are now on their own,
and free to roam,
in the Southwestern desert they call home.

CPSIA information can be obtained
at www.ICGtesting.com
Printed in the USA
LVHW071814180123
737415LV00011B/500